ID0821012

Searchlight BOOKS™

What Can We Learn from Early Civilizations?

Tools and Treasures of

Ancient Rome

Matt Doeden

Lerner Publications Company
Minneapolis

Lerner Publications Company
A division of Lerner Publishing Group, Inc.
241 First Avenue North
Minneapolis, MN 55401 U.S.A.

For reading levels and more information, look up this title at www.lernerbooks.com.

Library of Congress Cataloging-in-Publication Data

Doeden, Matt.
    Tools and treasures of ancient Rome / by Matt Doeden.
        pages   cm. — (Searchlight books™—What can we learn from early civilizations?)
    Includes index.
    ISBN 978–1–4677–1433–4 (lib. bdg. : alk. paper)
    ISBN 978–1–4677–2508–8 (eBook)
    1. Rome—Civilization—Juvenile literature. I. Title.
DG77.D64 2014
937'.63—dc23   2013022290

Manufactured in the United States of America
1 – PC – 12/31/13

Contents

Chapter 1

THE ANCIENT ROMANS

Almost three thousand years ago, a small village formed in present-day Italy. At first, Rome was like any other village in the area. But it soon became the center of one of Europe's greatest civilizations. Rome changed the world in many ways. Its people left behind amazing tools and treasures.

Rome was not always a huge, crowded city. What was it like in its early years?

The Rise of Rome

Rome started as a simple farming village. It sat near the Tiber River at a spot that was easy to cross. Travelers and traders often stopped there. Soon, Rome grew into a busy city.

The Tiber River runs through the heart of modern Rome.

Around 500 BCE, Rome formed a government called a republic. Landowners chose some men to make laws. These men were called senators.

Rome began taking over other lands. Soon the Romans controlled most of present-day Italy.

This marble statue from 270 CE shows Roman senators.

Ancient Rome

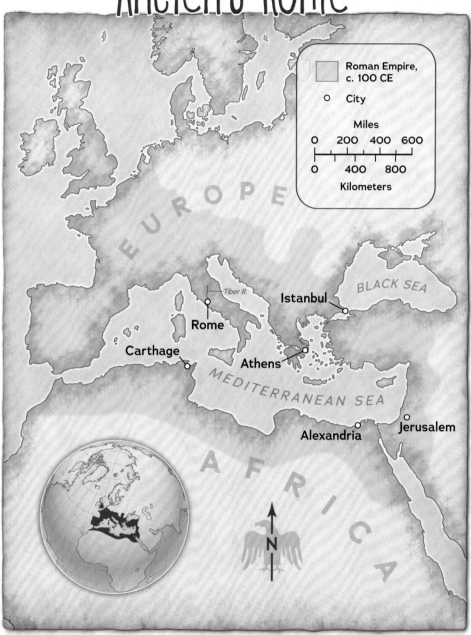

Roman Empire, c. 100 CE

City

Miles

0   200   400   600

0   400   800

Kilometers

EUROPE

BLACK SEA

Tiber R.

Istanbul

Rome

Carthage

Athens

MEDITERRANEAN SEA

Alexandria

Jerusalem

AFRICA

N

In 27 BCE, Augustus became Rome's first emperor. He ruled all the lands Rome had conquered. These lands were called the Roman Empire. During Augustus's rule, the empire grew even stronger. It spread to Europe, Africa, and Asia. Rome was the most powerful civilization in the world.

Emporer Augustus ruled Rome for more than forty years.

Chapter 2

DAILY LIFE

The Romans were proud of their civilization. They believed they were better than any other people. They worked hard to support the empire.

Classes

Each person in the Roman Empire had a specific role. Landowners made up the highest class of people. They were wealthier than most Romans. Some landowners even became senators. They made laws to govern the empire.

This Roman landowner holds busts of two relatives. How were landowners different from other Romans?

Most Romans were commoners. They worked as farmers, builders, and craftsmen. Their lives were centered on family. Aunts, uncles, grandparents, and other relatives often lived together in one home. The oldest father was in charge.

THIS URN SHOWS A ROMAN FAMILY EATING A MEAL.

Women had to obey their fathers and husbands. But Roman women had more rights than women in many other ancient cultures. Roman women could own property. They could divorce their husbands. Some Roman women even gave men advice about how to run the government.

This statue from about 5O CE shows a young Roman woman.

This mosaic from 150 CE
shows a Roman slave.

Slaves were the lowest class. Most slaves came from outside the Roman Empire. Romans bought slaves from other civilizations. They also captured enemies in battle and brought them home as slaves.

Slaves had to do the hardest, most dangerous jobs. Most got no pay. But some slave owners treated their slaves like family. They gave their slaves gifts. Some paid their slaves or even set them free.

Freed slaves were called freedmen. They formed their own class. Most became merchants. They bought and sold goods in markets. Some freedmen grew very rich. But they were not allowed to become senators.

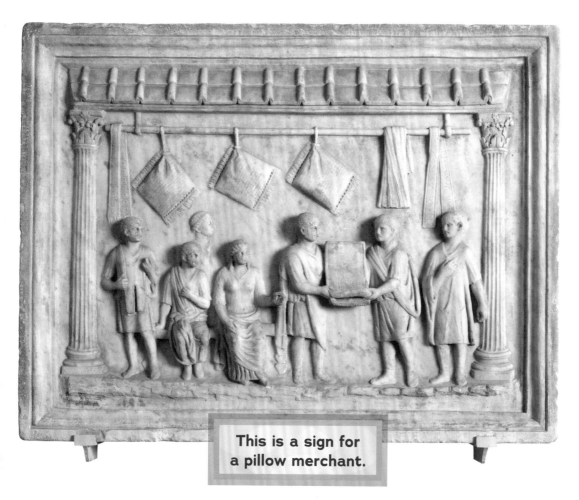

This is a sign for a pillow merchant.

Work

Rome started as a farming community. So farming was always important to the Romans. Farmers grew wheat and other grains. They also grew fruits and vegetables, including carrots, peas, grapes, and apricots. Farmers used plows pulled by oxen to break up the soil for planting. They used blades called sickles to harvest the crops.

This bronze statue of a man plowing is from around 550 BCE.

**Food from farms was
sold by traders in cities.**

Other Romans worked as craftspeople, architects, or builders. Traders bought food from farmers and sold it at busy markets.

Some Roman men worked as full-time soldiers. They fought with spears, swords, and shields.

ROMAN SOLDIERS CARRIED SPEARS AND SHIELDS AND WORE SHORT SWORDS AT THEIR WAISTS.

Communication

The people of the Roman Empire spoke many languages. But Latin was Rome's main language. In modern times, no one uses Latin as a main language. But Latin is still taught in some schools. It is used by many Christian churches. And it forms the roots of many modern languages, such as Italian and Spanish.

The Latin alphabet has twenty-two letters. The Romans spread this alphabet around parts of Asia, Africa, and Europe. Many modern alphabets, including the English alphabet, are based on it.

This piece of stone shows what Latin writing looks like.

Religion

Romans believed in many gods. Their gods looked and acted like humans. But the Romans thought these gods controlled everything that happened— from how often it rained to whether a person got sick.

Romans also believed the gods wanted Rome to rule the world. That was partly why Romans conquered so many other cultures.

Mars was the Roman god of war. He was one of the most powerful Roman gods.

Eventually, many people stopped believing in the gods. They still went to religious festivals and ceremonies. But fewer Romans really thought the gods controlled their world.

Starting in the first century CE, a new religion called Christianity swept through Rome. It became Rome's official religion in the 300s.

Early Christians painted this picture of Jesus near Rome.

Chapter 3

THE CULTURE OF ANCIENT ROME

The Romans borrowed many ideas from the cultures they conquered. They mixed these ideas together to create Roman art, architecture, and traditions. This formed a rich, unique culture.

Art

Romans loved art. They based many of their styles on ancient Greek art. Painters used bright colors to create images of gods, people, and animals. Many Romans liked paintings that showed scenes of peaceful farming life.

A Roman artist created this mosaic of a duck. What else did ancient Romans show in their art?

Roman sculptors also copied Greek styles. Sculptors carved everything from small figurines to life-sized images to stone reliefs. Reliefs were slabs of stone with carved figures that stood out from a flat background.

This relief shows people at a hairdresser.

Romans also loved crafts. They made fine jewelry from gold and bronze. Beautiful vases were made of glass. Everyday items such as knives and combs were often carved of bone.

THESE VASES WERE MADE AROUND 50 CE.

This is a modern re-creation of a Roman lyre.

We don't know what Roman music sounded like. But we know what instruments Romans played. Wind instruments included flutes, brass horns, and reed pipes. Stringed instruments such as the lyre were popular too. Drums and tambourines added a beat.

Architecture

The Romans were great engineers and architects. They built temples, palaces, arenas, and theaters. Common building materials included stone, brick, and concrete.

The Colosseum is one of Rome's most famous buildings. It is a giant arena.

The Pantheon is a famous Roman building that is known for its domed ceiling.

Many Roman buildings shared common features. Large columns and arches supported stone ceilings. Some buildings had curved ceilings called domes. Many buildings even had running water!

The Romans also built waterways called aqueducts. These channels carried freshwater into the city and took waste out of it. Some aqueducts were as long as 60 miles (97 kilometers)!

Romans built aqueducts all over the empire. This one is in modern-day France.

Pastimes

Romans had many kinds of entertainment. They enjoyed sports such as chariot races. Racers rode in small horse-drawn carts. Some chariots were pulled by as many as ten horses!

This relief shows a chariot race at the famous Circus Maximus.

At arenas such as the Colosseum, trained fighters called gladiators battled to the death. Thousands of Romans gathered to watch. Gladiators fought animals, criminals, and one another. Most gladiators were slaves. But if they won enough matches, they could earn their freedom.

Mosaics such as this one from the 300s show gladiators fighting animals.

Actors rehearse a play.

Romans also loved the theater. They borrowed plays from the ancient Greeks. Romans usually liked to watch comedies. These plays have happy endings. Tragedies were less popular. Their endings are sad.

Many Romans enjoyed bathhouses. People gathered there to bathe, exercise, talk with friends, and relax. Bathhouses had libraries full of books. Musicians and actors performed on stages inside bathhouses. No one got bored while washing up!

This is the main bathing room of a Roman bathhouse.

Roman Legend

The Rise of Rome

Rome's beginning is wrapped in legend. Romans told this story about how their city started.

Romulus and Remus were twin brothers. Their father was the god Mars. Their mother was the daughter of a king who had lost his kingdom. The new king feared that the boys would someday claim their grandfather's throne. So he ordered a servant to put the babies into a basket. The servant placed the basket in the Tiber River. The king hoped the boys would drown.

But the basket washed ashore. A female wolf found the babies and kept them safe. Later, a shepherd and his wife raised them.

When the brothers grew up, they wanted to start a city in the place where the wolf had found them. The land there was covered by hills. The brothers decided to build their city on one of these hills. But they couldn't agree on which hill to choose. They fought. Romulus won. He built his city on the hill he liked. This was the beginning of Rome.

Chapter 4

THE FALL OF ROME

The Roman Empire was powerful for hundreds of years. It grew and grew. But not everyone liked being part of the empire. Conquered people were forced to copy Roman ways. They were punished if they didn't follow the Roman religion. They also had to pay taxes to the emperor.

Some of these conquered people fought back. The empire was at war with itself.

Many Roman reliefs show soldiers in battle. Why did people fight against the Roman empire?

The End of an Era

In 117 CE, Emperor Hadrian came to power. Hadrian realized the empire had to stop growing. It was becoming too big to control. There weren't enough Roman soldiers to stop all the rebels. And it took too long for messages to travel across the empire. So Hadrian pulled his armies back. But this didn't help. The empire grew weaker and weaker.

EMPEROR HADRIAN WAS IN POWER UNTIL 138 CE.

In 330, Emperor Constantine moved the empire's capital to Istanbul. He renamed the city Constantinople. In 364, the empire split in two. Rome ruled the western half. Constantinople ruled the east.

This painting of Constantinople was created in the 1800s.

Roman soldiers battle their German enemies in this relief.

Meanwhile, Rome was under attack. Armies from Persia and Germany invaded. In 476, a German army defeated the Romans. The Roman Empire was gone.

Rome Today

The Roman Empire fell. But the city of Rome and its people remained. Present-day Rome is home to more than 2 million people. Many of them are descendants of the ancient Romans.

Many people come to Rome to see the Pantheon.

Millions of tourists visit Rome each year. People flock to see its ancient art and architecture. The treasures of Rome remind them of the great empire that began there thousands of years ago.

The Forum was a gathering place at the center of ancient Rome.

Glossary

aqueduct: a waterway built by humans to carry water from one place to another

arch: a curved structure often used to support the weight of a bridge or a roof

chariot: a small wheeled vehicle pulled by a horse

civilization: a large society in which people share a common government and culture

conquer: to take over a land by force

dome: a rounded vault that forms the roof of a building

empire: a large group of states or nations under a single leader

gladiator: a person trained to fight in an arena for entertainment

plow: a tool used to cut, lift, and turn over soil before planting crops

rebel: a person who fights against the government

relief: a carving featuring figures that stand out from a flat background

republic: a system of government in which power is held by the people, through elected representatives

senator: an elected official whose job is to make laws and help govern a realm

tax: a payment owed to a government

LERNER e SOURCE™

Expand learning beyond the printed book. Download free, complementary educational resources for this book from our website, www.lerneresource.com.

Learn More about Ancient Rome

Books

Ganeri, Anita. *How the Ancient Romans Lived*. New York: Gareth Stevens, 2011. Discover more about daily life in ancient Rome, from food and drink to entertainment.

Innes, Brian. *Ancient Roman Myths*. New York: Gareth Stevens, 2010. The ancient Romans told many myths to explain everyday events. Learn more about these fascinating stories.

Rice, Rob S. *Ancient Roman Warfare*. Pleasantville, NY: GS Learning Library, 2009. War was a big part of life in ancient Rome. Discover the weapons and tactics Roman armies used.

Sonneborn, Liz. *The Romans: Life in Ancient Rome*. Minneapolis: Lerner Publications, 2010. Discover surprising details about ancient Roman daily activities, ideas, and accomplishments.

Steele, Philip. *The Roman Empire*. New York: Rosen, 2009. Learn more about the rise and fall of one of the world's great civilizations.

Websites

BBC Primary History: Romans
http://www.bbc.co.uk/schools/primaryhistory/romans
This site, designed for kids, explores many aspects of ancient Rome, from technology to religion.

HowStuffWorks: Rome and the Roman Empire
http://history.howstuffworks.com/ancient-rome/rome-and-the-roman-empire.htm
This information-packed site examines the geography, culture, and people of ancient Rome.

NG Kids: Ten Facts about the Ancient Romans
http://ngkids.co.uk/cool_stories/1226/10_facts_about_the_ancient_romans
Check out this site for some fun facts about ancient Rome.

PBS: The Roman Empire in the First Century
http://www.pbs.org/empires/romans
PBS offers a detailed look at the height of the Roman Empire, with a virtual library, maps, and much more.

Index

Photo Acknowledgments

The images in this book are used with the permission of: © Meshaphoto/E+/Getty Images, p. 4; © Goran Boglcevic/Dreamstime.com, p. 5; © DEA/G. Dagli Orti/De Agostini/Getty Images, pp. 6, 18, © Laura Westlund/Independent Picture Service, p. 7; © Yiannis Papadimitrio/Dreamstime.com, p. 8; © Leemage/Universal Image Group/Getty Images, p. 9; © Museo della Civilta Romana, Rome, Italy/ Giraudon/The Bridgeman Art Library, p. 10; The Granger Collection, New York, pp. 11, 23 © Chris Heller/ CORBIS, p. 12; © Alinari/Art Resource, NY, p. 13; © Museo Nazionale di Villa Giulia, Rome, Italy/The Bridgeman Art Library p. 14; © Erich Lessing/Art Resource, NY, p. 15; © DEA/A.Dagli Orti/De Agostini/ Getty Images, p. 16; © Vito Acromano/Alamy, p. 17; © Culture Club/Hulton Archive/Getty Images, p. 19; © Ray Roberts/Alamy, p. 20; © Visual Arts Library/The Bridgeman Art Library Ltd./Alamy, p. 21; © Museo Archeologico Nazionale, Aquileia, Italy/Giraudon/The Bridgeman Art Library, p. 22; © iStockphoto.com/haoliang, p. 24; © iStockphoto/Thinkstock, p. 25; © iStockphoto.com/Espiegle, p. 26; © De Agostini Picture Library/The Bridgeman Art Library, p. 27; © Alfredo Degli Orti/Art Resource, NY, p. 28; © Museo Archeologico Nazionale, Naples, Italy/Alinari/The Bridgeman Art Library, p. 29; © 1st Century/De Agostini Picture Library/G. Dagli OrtiThe Bridgeman Art Library, p. 30; © Roman/ The Bridgeman Art Library/Getty Images, p. 31; © Ancient Art and Architecture/Alamy, p. 32; © Time Life Pictures/Getty Images, p. 33; © Roberts, David (1796-1864)/Private Collection/The Bridgeman Art Library, p. 34; Jastrow/Wikimedia Commons, p. 35; © Honzahruby/Dreamstime.com, p. 36; © Peter Phipp/Photolibrary/Getty Images, p. 37.

Front cover: © Roman/The Bridgeman Art Library/Getty Images.

Main body text set in Adrianna Regular 14/20. Typeface provided by Chank.